2026

The College Survival Guide For Your Son

LEVEL UP YOUR INDEPENDENCE

Copyright

Copyright © 2026 by RK Publishing LLC
All rights reserved.

No part of this publication may be reproduced, distributed, or transmitted in any form or by any means, including photocopying, recording, or other electronic or mechanical methods, without prior written permission of the author, except in the case of brief quotations used in reviews or scholarly work, with proper citation.

Paperback ISBN: 979-8-9948353-0-2

Printed in the United States of America.
Third Edition

PREFACE

Letting him go is one of the hardest things you'll ever do. Helping him be ready makes it a little easier. College marks the moment your son steps into his own life—new responsibilities, new freedoms, and new challenges he'll face without you right down the hall. This guide is here to bridge that space between who he's been and who he's becoming.

Inside, you'll find simple, confidence-building chapters that help him:

• Prepare for the transition before he leaves home
• Handle the everyday tasks you've quietly done for years
• Cook a few meals, clean a space, manage laundry, and stay organized
• Take care of himself so he can focus on what truly matters—growing, learning, and finding his place in the world.

This isn't just a book about surviving college.
It's a gentle handoff.

A way to say, "You've got this—and I've prepared you well."
Give him the tools. Trust his wings. Watch him rise.

Guide to Kicking Butt in College (and Beyond)

Introduction: So, You're Leveling Up.

Look, the world's changed. You know it, your parents know it. College isn't just a place to hit the books; it's a trial by fire, a proving ground where you learn to stand on your own two feet, maybe for the first time. We're not talking about your grandpappy's college days or even twenty years ago. The stakes are higher, the costs are steeper, and the world outside these dorm walls is waiting to see what you're made of.

I've seen hundreds of new recruits—yeah, *recruits*, because that's what you are—come through these gates, eager, terrified, and sometimes, totally unprepared. I've spent years in the trenches, helping students navigate the chaos, from crushing exams to that first terrifying load of laundry. And I've seen the ones who figure it out, the ones who don't just survive, but *thrive*. They learn the ropes, they get smart, and they emerge ready for anything. This guide? This is their playbook.

This isn't your grandma's advice column. This is about real-world skills: how to keep your space from becoming a biohazard, how to dress like you mean business (even if you're just going to class), how to feed yourself something other than instant noodles, and how to conquer the laundry monster. More than that, it's about building the self-reliance that'll make your parents damn proud and set *you* up for a lifetime of success. It's about taking ownership of your life, learning to hustle, and understanding that independence doesn't mean isolation—it means knowing when to lean on your support system and when to stand tall on your own.

Let's be real. Many of you have had it pretty good. Your parents smoothed out the rough edges, picked up the slack, and probably fought battles you didn't even know were happening. And hats off to them – they got you here, ready for the next challenge. But now? It's your turn. This guide starts where they left off, handing you the torch. They've done their part; now it's time to show them what they raised.

From firsthand experience, I'm telling you: nothing tanks your reputation faster than being "that kid"—the one who smells like a locker room, lives in a disaster zone, or constantly mooches off everyone else. It's not just embarrassing; it's a weakness. This guide gives you the intel to avoid those rookie mistakes. It's common sense, sure, but common sense isn't always common practice when you're overwhelmed and on your own.

Whether you crack this open before you pack your bags, the moment you hit campus, or when you're elbow-deep in your first laundry catastrophe, keep it. Use it. This isn't just a guide; it's your tactical advantage. And trust me, it's going to help you dominate these next few years of your life.

2026 Guide to College Survival

Table of Contents

College Survival Guide For Sons ....

Copyright ....

PREFACE ....

Chapter 1: Prepare for Launch 1

    Getting Ready to Go... Mentally and Physically 1

    Engaging Mental Grit Mode 2

    Fortifying Physical Fortitude 3

Chapter 2: Tactical Plan 5

    Operation: Leave the Nest (and take their money) 5

    Student's Solo Prep List (Your Mission Brief) 6

    The Uniform (3-Season Wardrobe) 8

    Parent-Funded Supply Lists (The Loot) 9

Chapter 3: Immediate Deployment 12

    Operation: Secure the Territory 12

Chapter 4: Co-Existence or Mutually Assured Destruction 14

    Roommates: Surviving the Social Grind 14

Chapter 5: Dorm Life: Survival in the Concrete Jungle 17

    Mastering Collegiate Housing Without Getting Evicted 17

Chapter 6: Operation: De-Stinkification 19

    Proper Hygiene for Young Adults (Stop Being Gross) 19

Chapter 7: The Cash Flow Battle 22
   Making and Spending Money (Stop Being a Freeloader) 22

Chapter 8: Culinary and Cleanliness Combat.............................25
   Groceries, Cooking, Cleaning, and the Laundry Gauntlet......25
   Cleaning: Stop Living Like a Pig 27
   Fluff, Fold, and Store (Look Like a Professional) 30
   Kitchen Combat: Essential Cooking Tips 33

Quick Meals in Minutes 39
   Meals in 5 Minutes..39
   Meals in 10 Minutes..42
   Meals in 20 Minutes..48

Chapter 1: Prepare for Launch

Getting Ready to Go... Mentally and Physically

You got the letter. You're in. That acceptance means two things: First, you're finally going to college. Second, your real life is about to start, and guess what? **It's going to be terrifying.**

For the first time, you are launching yourself into the wild. You'll be navigating a new city, a new school, and a massive horde of new people who don't know your history. This isn't just about moving your stuff; it's about becoming responsible for yourself, your schedule, your food, and your laundry (yes, actual laundry). It is a **constant, exhausting juggling act**. You need to get organized, gather your battle gear, and execute a flawless exit strategy. You chose this path—the path of a professional, the path to the big, scary world. It's not easy, but you're not fragile. You can do this. This guide is your tactical briefing.

In this chapter, we're doing a mandatory pre-flight check on three critical systems before you touch down on campus:

1. **Mental Grit:** Shutting down the fear and prepping your brain to handle the shock of independence.
2. **Physical Fortitude:** Protecting your health and preparing your body for the environmental and social grind.
3. **Tactical Logistics:** Assembling the necessary supplies to avoid a day-one panic attack.

Engaging Mental Grit Mode

Leaving the 'rents is epic. It's scary, life-changing, and the biggest shot of freedom you've ever had. So, here's the mandate: **Enjoy it.** Study like your scholarship depends on it, work hard to build your future, and have fun like it's your job. That's what being a college student and an adult is all about. Get hyped. Go **100% on everything**. Half-assing it belongs in high school.

Mentally, you're leaving your home base—the only place where someone routinely asked if you ate a vegetable. You're leaving your friends and the people who literally kept you alive for the last two decades. Remember how your parents tried to teach you basic survival skills like cleaning your room, doing dishes, or achieving self-sufficiency? You, like every other ambitious teen, ignored all that because you were too busy crushing the ACT/PSAT, playing games, or working a summer job that you probably spent more time complaining about than working.

You never really thanked them for picking up the slack, did you? Don't sweat it. They'll forgive you if you get your act together *now* and make a clean break. Take all that mental effort you spent agonizing over grades and redirect it to a single, critical mission: **Surviving the first term.**

This is the time for mental toughness. Prove every doubter—including the tiny, nervous voice inside your own head—that you're tough enough to leave the nest, take on the world, and make a dent in it. Be relentless. Stay positive. Network.

And, for God's sake, have some fun.

Fortifying Physical Fortitude

You are stepping into a hostile new environment filled with thousands of different people and huge physical variables. You're not just emotionally affected; your body is about to take a hit.

- **Altitude, Humidity, and Allergens:** Is your new campus 5,000 feet higher? Near a swamp? Suddenly surrounded by oak trees? These changes will mess with you. **Look into these variables now.**
- **The Insurance Battle Plan:** You will get sick. You will trip. You will need a dentist eventually. If you're still on your parents' plan, immediately identify the nearest in-network doctor and dentist. If you don't have insurance, stop reading and get some. Seriously. It is that important. You don't want to start your adult life with a five-figure medical bill for a three-day flu. You might have to choose between a Netflix streaming bundle or medical coverage. **Choose the coverage.** It sits right at the top of the priority list. Carry that insurance card—it's useless if it's in a filing cabinet back home.

Physically, your new room and campus will feel alien. The furniture is wrong; the layout is weird. But adjustment is surprisingly fast. Once you actually **organize your room** and establish some semblance of a **schedule** (even a messy one), that feeling of control kicks in. Freedom is great, but only when you're responsible enough to handle the chaos it generates.

You are now the CEO of You Inc. Take ownership of your name and make it mean something good. Be decent, be honest, and definitely be competitive. You'll meet future friends, rivals, and maybe even a few enemies. Follow this eternal rule: **Never burn a bridge.** That person you slighted in the study group might be your superior someday. Don't be an idiot.

Finally, living in a shoebox with another human is a major physical and mental shift. Chapter 4 will give you the essential tactics for not throttling your roommate and keeping the peace through communication and acceptance. Consider it your guide to basic cohabitation survival.

Chapter 2: Tactical Plan

Operation: Leave the Nest (and take their money)

Alright, fresh meat. You've accepted the psychological reality (Chapter 1), but now it's time to get *tactical*. Hope isn't a strategy; a plan is. Starting today, your life is an endless cascade of lists. You have approximately two weeks to a month to shop, pack, and coordinate your entire damn life. This isn't a fun road trip; it's a military deployment.

Mission: Exploit Your Parents (Tactical Financial Acquisition)

Listen up. Your parents, despite all the complaining (or over-celebrating) about you leaving, are your greatest asset right now. If you have been an absolute dumpster fire of a human lately, you need to mend those bridges *immediately*. Your family is the only lifeline you can 100% count on.

Execution Protocol:

1. **Grovel:** If you were a menace, apologize. Buy the rose. Promise, maybe lie, that you will never do it again.
2. **The Drop:** Wait a few days for the good vibes to set in. Then, gently present your *shopping list* (provided at the end of this chapter).
3. **The Divide and Conquer:** Don't hand them a scroll that looks like the Declaration of Independence. If the list is a nightmare, break it down into

manageable weekly chunks. "Mom, would you mind grabbing a few basic survival items next time you're at Target?" (Translation: You are now funding my dorm room.)

Now that the supply chain is secured with Mom and Dad footing the bill for necessities, *your* job is to impress them with organized action. Here is your personal to-do list:

Student's Solo Prep List (Your Mission Brief)

1. The Paperwork Grunt Work

- **Confirm Everything (Again):** Call the school. Check loans, scholarships, and boarding info. Pretend you're a paranoid auditor. **Free Money Alert:** You are still eligible for scholarships. Stop being lazy. It takes minutes a week to apply for that sweet, sweet cash. Do it.

2. Cash Flow and Labor

- **Get a Job:** Start calling for part-time work near campus. **Prioritize work-study programs.** They are easier to snag, but it's first-come, first-served. Be proactive. Get names. Get phone numbers. Have a resume ready to deploy. You need cash for late-night pizza and other "necessities."

3. Reconnaissance

- **Campus Tour & Enrollment Prep:** Go tour the campus if you haven't. Get familiar. Research classes. When enrollment day hits, **go early** and be prepared. Do not be the confused idiot wandering into the wrong lecture hall.

4. Logistics (The Move)

- **Vehicle Check:** Get your car serviced and detailed. If you don't have a car, secure transportation. If you can't borrow a truck, know that rental trucks are surprisingly cheap for small loads ($25–35, plus gas). **Save some of that summer job cash for the U-Haul.**

5. Tactical Comfort Acquisition

- **Buy Happiness:** Start shopping for dorm upgrades. Soup warmers, hot plates, small microwave (check your dorm rules first—don't get kicked out on day one!), toasters, small fridges. Anything that lets you make real snacks instead of surviving solely on overpriced cafeteria sludge. Grab a beanbag chair. Ask nicely for any housewares your parents are willing to sacrifice. They are so proud right now, they'll probably hand over the family silver.
Ask for it!

The Uniform (3-Season Wardrobe)

This is college, not a fashion show (mostly). But you can't be a slob.

- **Socks & Underwear:** Buy new ones. **Do not** let your mother pick these out unless you are physically present. No one wants to wear someone else's idea of comfortable underwear.
- **The Laundry Gauntlet: DO ALL YOUR LAUNDRY.** If you don't know how, stop what you are doing, flip to Chapter 8, and learn. Now.
- **Sorting:** Once clean, sort your wardrobe into three stacks next to your bags (Spring/Fall, Winter, Summer).
    - **Basics:** 10–15 pairs of socks (get variety), 10 T-shirts, Short Sleeve and Long Sleeve. Several jeans/shorts.
    (Remember: College, not a yacht cruise.)
    - **Smart Clothes:** Stylish walking shoes, a couple of "nice" outfits.
    - **Survival Gear:** PJ pants, a robe, all-weather coats (the kind with detachable arms/lining/Waterproof windbreaker), and cold-weather accessories (hats, gloves) especially if you're moving north.

Packing Up

- **The Bags:** You need serious containers. Big army duffel bags from a surplus store or Salvation Army are cheap, tough, and double perfectly as laundry bags.
- **The Buffer Week:** Keep out a week's worth of clothes you don't care about. Pack the rest. This

way, you don't have to do laundry the week before you leave. When you come home for break, maybe, just maybe, someone will have magically washed the scraps you left behind. (Don't count on it, but hope is nice.)

Parent-Funded Supply Lists (The Loot)

Category	Must-Haves (Make Mom Buy)	Your Extras (If possible
Academic Gear	**Backpack (Don't skimp—get thick, padded straps! Lots of pockets of different sizes.)**	Laptop/Printer
	Pencils, Pens, Erasers, Notebooks, Calculator	Pocket Recorder for lectures
	Tape, Stapler, 3-Hole Punch, Ruler, Post-Its	**Duct Tape, Rope** (You'll need them.)

Hygiene	Soap, Shampoo, **Deodorant (Triple supply!),** Toothbrushes/Paste/Floss, Razors, Shaving Cream	Electric Shaver And beard trimmer. Nose and ear hair trimmer
Dorm Life	2 sets of Bedding & Pillowcases (Go with them to buy!)	Towels, Washcloths, Robe, Slippers, Rugs
Extras	Cork Board for schedules/photos, Plastic glasses/plates/utensils	Shelving (bricks and boards), Hot Plate/Toaster/Microwave, Small Fridge
Electronics/Money	Anything you can get them to contribute	Stereo/iPad, TV/Game Console, Cell Phone, **Credit Card ($200 emergency limit)**

Travel/Misc	N/A	Bicycle & lock, long board, electric scooter.

It looks like a mountain of stuff, but most of it is probably collecting dust in your house. The better your relationship with your parents, the more they will surrender. Be nice, be strategic. Buy cheap for essentials (Walmart/Target) and let your parents take you to the fancy stores for clothes and expensive gear.

Now that the shelves are stocked and your plan is in motion, it's time to pack and adjust to the emotional and physical reality of leaving. Head to the next chapter to learn how to keep your sanity during this whole messy, wonderful process.

Chapter 3: Immediate Deployment

Operation: Secure the Territory

Listen up. You've hauled your stuff, you've kissed your parents goodbye (or at least offered a firm nod), and you're standing in your new, tiny, glorified closet. Now is not the time to unpack leisurely or cry. This is the time for **immediate action.**

Your First Directive: Move Fast. Go early, register early, and get your bearings *fast*.

1. Register and Learn the Surroundings

- **Lock it Down:** Even if you pre-registered, confirm everything. If you haven't registered, drop your bags and go *now*. Do not pass Go, do not collect $200.
- **Find Your Class Locations:** Once registered, take a hard-core, tactical tour of the campus. **Locate every single classroom and lecture hall** you need. Don't rely on some map app you've never used. Physically walk the routes. The first day of class is not the time to be sprinting across campus, sweating and confused.

2. The First Impression Blitz

- **Be the Early Bird:** Be early to every class. Not just on time—**early**. This is non-negotiable. Falling behind in college is like falling into quicksand; it happens fast and

pulls you under hard. Showing up early ensures you get a decent seat, don't miss any critical first-day instructions, and, yes, it makes you look like a motivated student to your instructor. Use that to your advantage.
- **Network (Don't Be a Hermit):** This isn't high school. Use every single opportunity to introduce yourself and state your interests. Making friends is difficult, but it's easier when you're not an invisible wallflower. You'd be surprised how many people are into the exact same niche weirdness you are. **Spread your wings and make some noise.**

3. Identity and Adaptation

- **Evolve, Don't Follow:** College is your ultimate testing ground. This is the time to explore who you are, what you stand for, and what opinions you can defend. **Develop your own damn opinions and think for yourself.** The time for being a passive follower is over. Be a leader. All the cheesy clichés apply here, so stop being embarrassed and just **be yourself.**
- **The Plan B Mandate:** If Plan A (the classes, the friends, the routine) starts to crash and burn, don't sulk. **Initiate Plan B.** That's life. Get used to pivoting. If something isn't working, change it. College is a constant process of adaptation. Those who adjust quickly survive; those who cling to old habits drown.

Chapter 4: Co-Existence or Mutually Assured Destruction

Roommates: Surviving the Social Grind

Welcome to the ultimate freshman test: The roommate. For the next nine months, you're stuck in a twelve-by-fifteen foot cell with a complete stranger pulled from some random corner of the map. They might be your future best man, or they might be a human experiment in chaos. Either way, this is the biggest social issue you'll face.

This chapter is your combat guide for roommates—how to survive them, how to fix them, and how to file the necessary paperwork for a swift extraction if needed. (Later chapters cover lesser horrors like hygiene and shared ramen noodles.)

Embrace the Freak Flag (Initial Assessment)

When you pull people from all 50 states and drop them into a dorm, you get weirdness. Different diets, different music, different smells. **Your job is to embrace the differences and stop building walls.**

The person across the room is getting an education just like you are. Period. They can wear weird clothes, have hair down to their knees, and drink milk with their feet—it doesn't matter. **Acceptance rules the day.** If you focus on what's inside (i.e., whether they're fundamentally decent), 90% of your problems disappear.

Sometimes, the weird behavior isn't malicious; it's just awkwardness. Maybe they have ADHD, maybe they are cripplingly shy. Don't pile on the abuse. Try to understand and offer a helpful suggestion. Let them know it's okay to have a different opinion and use their voice. **College is the perfect place to let that freak flag fly.** Don't just go along with the crowd; be creative, make changes, and use your voice. We need that for a brighter future—and that process starts with getting along in this tiny room.

Handling Conflict (The Gauntlet)

Let's be real. Sometimes you get a problem: The Bully, The Thief (who eats all your food), or The Slob. You cannot just "put up with it."

1. **Direct Communication (The Talk):** Try to work it out first. Talk to them. Offer alternatives ("Hey, I use those snacks for class—maybe we split the grocery bill?"). **Remember: "You always get more with honey."**
2. **Peer Intervention (Call in Reinforcements):** If talking fails, call a mutual friend to intervene.
3. **The Nuclear Option (RA):** If it gets completely out of control, you go straight to the **Resident Advisor (RA)** and change rooms. You deserve better than daily chaos.

The Bully Dilemma:

I've seen strong bonds forged in roommate fire, and I've seen friendships destroyed. If you have a bigger person picking on a smaller person, brute force is for idiots. **Talking it out is the smarter move.** Often, understanding *why* the behavior is happening can flip the script, and they end up becoming friends.

But if you see someone getting picked on or taken advantage of—**you have a moral obligation to intervene.** Say something. If you stand by silently, you are just as much to blame. You'll want someone to stick up for you someday, right? Start building that karma now.

Emergency Ejection Protocol

Most issues are resolved with a conversation and some ground rules. But some cannot be. **If you feel threatened in any way, physically or emotionally, you get out immediately.** Abusive behavior is a zero-tolerance offense on any college campus. Go directly to a **Student Advisor** or the RA for solutions *before* the situation escalates. Your safety and sanity are not negotiable.

Chapter 5: Dorm Life: Survival in the Concrete Jungle

Mastering Collegiate Housing Without Getting Evicted

Listen up. You're now a resident of the dorms—a cramped, communal, concrete fortress governed by bureaucratic rules and questionable plumbing. Your mission here is simple: **Do not be the problem.**

The housing authority might feel like the gestapo, but I'm telling you, 99% of the time, they are right. If you choose to go off-script, you are choosing trouble. The rules are there for one reason: to prevent mass chaos when you stick 500 teenagers in a building. **Just live by the rules and you will be fine.**

The Responsibility Mandate (Your Ownership)

Your college life starts *now*, and that means responsibility. You are not just responsible for your room; you are responsible for the entire neighborhood you inhabit.

- **Protect the Asset:** Learn to take care of the space. You're renting this, not destroying it. Keep the furniture intact for the next poor soul who has to live here.
- **The Smell Test:** Take ownership of your domain. Your room is a direct reflection of you, and trust me, "Slob" is not the unique, impressive definition you want. It's perfectly fine to be unique, artistic, or eclectic, as long

- as your "uniqueness" is orderly and, critically, **doesn't smell like a swamp.**
- **Pay the Toll:** Just do what you are asked and **get your payment in on time.** No one needs that financial headache.

The Neighborly Tactical Play

Want to throw a small party or just blast music while studying for a big test? Don't be a caveman. Being a decent human is the highest form of tactical advantage you have.

- **Ask the RA:** Always ask your Resident Advisor (RA) when having small gatherings.
- **Give Your Neighbors a Heads-Up:** Give advanced warning to neighbors if you're planning loud music on a particular night.

You'd be shocked how cool people are when you show a little basic courtesy. They'll be grateful you asked, rather than being jolted by a sudden flood of strangers or an impromptu bass solo at midnight. **Be courteous, keep your space clean, and the whole operation will be groovy.**

Ready to move on to the messy stuff: communal hygiene and sharing food?

Chapter 6:
Operation: De-Stinkification

Proper Hygiene for Young Adults (Stop Being Gross)

Let's address the elephant in the tiny, poorly ventilated room: You might stink.

If you notice your roommate recoiling, or if people instinctively stand six feet away from you (and not because of social anxiety), you have a problem. Proper hygiene isn't optional in a tight college environment. One "stinker" ruins the air quality for everyone, turning your academic sanctuary into a biochemical hazard.

If your roommate smells like a compost heap, don't harass him—educate him. Believe me, he'd rather hear it from you than have a nervous professor deliver a diplomatic lecture on BO after class.

Stench Warfare Protocol (What Works, What's Nuclear)

- The Gentle Guide: Talk to him first. Offer alternatives. If he's stubborn, give him this chapter. Maybe seeing the rules in print will shame him into compliance.
- The Nuclear Option (Last Resort): If all else fails, you must revert to embarrassing battlefield tactics. Leaving

a fresh stick of deodorant prominently displayed on their desk, or strategically "misting" them with Febreze when they walk by. I've seen it work, but it's mean, messy, and totally avoidable if the offender just *listens*.

The Non-Negotiable Rules of Cleanliness

For whatever reason, some of you missed this life lesson growing up. This is your mandatory refresher:

1. Shower or Die (Daily): If you are not taking a shower *at least* every other day, you are failing. Adults need a daily rinse. If you are active (sports, running from your landlord), you need two. If you smell, for God's sake, take a shower. It's common sense, not rocket science.
2. The Deodorant Defensive: Use deodorant every day. Use it twice a day if you start smelling funky halfway through your 11 AM lecture. Bring it with you. Reapplying is a sign of a responsible adult, not a failure.
3. Scent Discipline: Aftershave and cologne are great tools, but use them sparingly. They are an accent, not a force field. Never, ever use cologne to cover up a smelly body. You don't smell better; you smell like a sweaty flower—it makes the problem worse.
4. Know Your Products: Stick to the soaps and shampoos you used at home. Switching brands can cause rashes and scalp chaos. After you scrub, use lotion. Dry, flaky skin doesn't make you tough; it makes you look like a lizard that hasn't found a watering hole.
5. Shave and Conquer: Shave as needed for whatever style you're going for. But pay attention to the back of your head. A hairy neck is unacceptable in any style. **Find** someone—a friend, a barber, a very brave roommate—

to shave that line so you don't look like an evolutionary missing link.
6. The Hand Inspection: Manicure your nails. Keep your fingers and toes clean and trimmed. Most of the germs you encounter are living under those things. People *always* look at hands; they are a critical first-impression tool. Make a good impression, not a gross one.

Chapter 7:
The Cash Flow Battle

Making and Spending Money (Stop Being a Freeloader)

Let's talk about the cold, hard truth: **Money is the ultimate college survival tool.**

If your parents aren't wiring you a stack of cash every Monday, you need a job—a work-study gig, a graveyard shift, whatever. That's the reality. I wrote this guide for survivors, not professional freeloaders. You *must* carry your own weight. Nothing sinks your social standing faster than being a mooch. People hate a freeloader. If you want to participate in the fun, you must contribute. I've watched good people become pariahs simply because they couldn't be bothered to get a part-time job.

Find a job. Take it. Whatever it is. Money equals cushion, and the more cushion you have, the easier it is to survive the inevitable punches college throws at you.

Get Off Your Ass and Get Hired

If you failed to plan ahead and secure a work-study job (as Chapter 2 suggested), then **change the damn plan.** You need every piece of paper currency you can get. Things are expensive now, and guess what? You buy them yourself.

- **No Excuses:** If you are wondering what "resources" you have, the answer is: *not enough.* Find a job.
- **Target the Big Fish:** Hit up the school employment office or career fairs. **Call UPS or FedEx.** They often offer great programs for students, including tuition reimbursement. It's hard labor, but it's a solid opportunity to earn cash and get some of your education debt paid for.
- **Be Proud, Not Picky:** There are tons of flexible jobs out there. **Don't be choosy.** Take the first decent paycheck you find and work your tail off. If that job ends up being a nightmare, quit and find a better one. That's life; get used to the grind.

Managing Your Loot (The $100/Week Challenge)

Once you're in a steady routine and the paychecks start rolling in, you need to manage the flow like a financial hawk.

1. **Bills Before Bites: Always pay bills first, and eat second.** Stress from overdue bills is a morale killer. Stay on top of your obligations to free up your mental energy for studying.
2. **The Budget Benchmark:** Minus housing costs, you absolutely can and should survive off **$100.00 a week.** That's only $400 a month. You can earn that working part-time for minimum wage anywhere. **There are no excuses.** Fail to do this, and you will become a mooch or you will starve.
3. **Frugal is the New Flex:** You need cash for groceries, gas, and those "extra" things (like video games, or replacing that thing your roommate broke). It is ten times easier to survive college with cash in your pocket. **Be frugal.**

> Only afford the luxuries you *must* have. Go without the rest. Your future self will thank you when you're not living paycheck to paycheck.

When you start paying your own way, you stop constantly "borrowing from Peter to pay Paul." Self-sufficiency is a powerful feeling. The sooner you realize this, the sooner you can stop stressing about money and buckle down on the only thing that actually matters: **your homework.**

I've even put together some simple, wallet-friendly recipes and shopping suggestions for you later in the book. It's your call: Take the advice and survive, or ignore it and struggle month after month. *Choose wisely.*

Chapter 8: Culinary and Cleanliness Combat

Groceries, Cooking, Cleaning, and the Laundry Gauntlet

Alright, listen up. You are 18–20 years old. Your primary function besides studying is **eating.** Food will be the biggest source of conflict, debt, and joy in your new life. You need a tactical plan for groceries, cooking, and stopping your roommate from eating your survival rations.

Groceries: The War of the Fridge

The refrigerator is a sacred, finite resource. You must establish rules *immediately*.

- **The Food Pact:** Get a written agreement. Seriously. Who is splitting the cost? How much is each person contributing? If you're keeping separate food, clearly divide the fridge and cabinet space. Mark your territory like a territorial animal.
- **The Shopping List (No Junk):** If you are splitting costs, agree on the list. Let everyone pick *one* indulgence (not a whole bag of Gumby snakes). The rest of the list must be common sense: good, healthy food that yields multiple meals. This is about survival, not satisfying a chip craving.

Cooking: Ditch the Dorm Sludge

You will inevitably crave a home-cooked meal. If you are cooking for yourself, you must learn the basics of self-survival.

- **Freeloading is Theft:** Food is precious. You only take what you put in. It is absolutely fine to keep track and pay someone back. Don't be a food freeloader. Feeding someone a couple of times is nice; constantly funding their diet is expensive and irritating. **Nicely ask them to contribute or hit the road.** They need to learn where the line is.
- **Survival Cooking:** You must learn to cook. This guide gives you quick hacks: how to bake a potato faster, flip an egg without a disaster, or cook a pizza without burning one half. Every shortcut helps.
- **Feed the Brain:** Being able to cook and maintain healthy habits is **Number One on the survival list.** If your body starves, your mind starves. Eat right, and everything else—your grades, your focus—improves. Variety and moderation are key.

Combatting the Freshman 15

Gaining weight your first year is notorious. Unless you are severely underweight, healthy eating and exercise are mandatory.

- **The Dorm Food Defense:** If you have cooking appliances (hot plate, microwave, etc.), use them. They are healthier than most cafeteria options. If you rely on dorm food, be smart:

- **Breakfast:** Fruits, yogurt, cereal. **Do not skip breakfast.** It is the most important meal of the day. A banana and a granola bar is the minimum insurance for a productive day.
- Most cafeterias offer a packed lunch to take on campus. Get it at breakfast and put it in your backpack. Saved my life in college for sure. Otherwise pack a snack for midday from your stash.
- **Ditch the Processed Crap:** Stay away from the mashed potatoes and gravy. That stuff goes straight to the thighs.
- **Hydration is Free:** Drink water. Lots of it. Loading up on milk in the morning from the cafeteria is free and good for the protein. **Soda is the leading cause of obesity.** Limit yourself to one soda a day, tops. Water is free and necessary for survival. Don't be a statistic.

Cleaning: Stop Living Like a Pig

This is the hard truth: **Cleaning up after yourself is not optional.**

If we all left our messes, this planet would be piled high with junk. Whether it's the kitchen, the bathroom, or the laundry room, **do not leave a mark behind.** Your future husband or wife will judge you harshly, so start practicing for the future now.

The Daily Pickup Drill (5 Minutes or Death)

- **The Put-Away Rule:** If you get something out, put it away. Immediately. Coats go in the closet. Shoes go away too. In a closet or under your bed.

- **First Impressions:** Keep the entry area clean. This habit will spread to other areas. Pick up daily, not weekly.
- **The Rodent Warning:** You must take out the trash **daily** to minimize insects and rodents. The number one attraction for pests is food left out. If you want to see maggots crawling out of your week-old garbage, keep ignoring this. Get a trash can with a lid.

The Hygiene Zone: Bathrooms

Nothing turns people off faster than a filthy bathroom. **This is non-negotiable.**

- **Clean it Often:** Anytime it *looks* dirty, wipe it down.
- **The Hairy, Yellow Stain Defense:** Nothing repels the opposite sex faster than a hairy, yellow-spotted toilet. It is disgusting and unacceptable. Wipe visible hair and spots with toilet paper throughout the week if necessary before your weekly cleaning.
- **The Weekly Deep Clean:** Scrub the entire toilet, inside and out (outside first). Don't forget the underside of the bowl. Clean the sink and wipe down the mirrors. **Clean the floors and rugs.** Germs brew here.

Cleaning Hacks

- **Soak the Disaster:** After a night of eating/partying, soak dirty dishes in hot, soapy water for at least a half hour before washing. This eliminates scrubbing. Plug the sink, fill it, and walk away. **Multi-task:** clean the rest of the room while the dishes soak!
- **No Mopping Up Their Mess:** If you end up being the only one who cleans, strike a deal. Volunteer to do the

cleaning, but negotiate a lower contribution to groceries or rent. **Do not let your roommates walk all over you.**

The Laundry Gauntlet

Yes, we're talking about laundry. Stop wearing the same smelly t-shirt for a week.

- **It's Not Hard:** It takes 30 minutes to wash and 40 minutes to dry. You can find one hour a week. No excuses for wearing stale underwear.
- **Sorting:** Colors in one pile (wash cold). Whites/Towels/Underwear in another (wash hot with a tiny bit of color-safe bleach to kill the germs).
- **Detergent Hack:** Only fill the detergent cup halfway. The line is there to make you buy more. The smaller the load the less detergent you need. Common sense.
- **The Wrinkle War: Take clothes out of the washer immediately.** Shake each piece, and throw them in the dryer. **Take them out of the dryer immediately** when done, shake them again and then lay them flat and fold them quickly after. If you follow this rule your clothes will be wrinkle free and you will rarely have to iron.

- **NOTE:** Do not overfill the washer. Only fill up about half way with dry clothes to ensure they get washed thoroughly.

Fluff, Fold, and Store (Look Like a Professional)

Taking clean clothes out of the dryer and throwing them into a pile doesn't cut it. Learn to fold properly:

- **T-Shirts:** Take them out hot, shake them and lay them flat. Fold arms in, and fold up from the bottom. This allows for neat stacking (like in the stores).

Lay shirt flat and fold in sides

Fold up from the bottom and stack

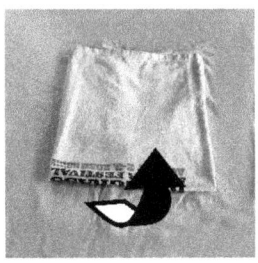 

> Lay the shirt flat and fold in the first sleeve, then down neatly. Repeat with second sleeve.

> Fold up from the bottom and stack

Pants: Shake them out, align the seams, run your hand down the legs to flatten, and use proper pant hangers to avoid wrinkles around the knees.

> Folding pants with no pleat

 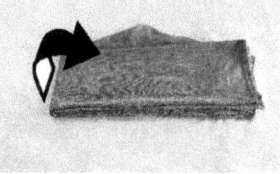

```
Folding pants with pleats

Line up seams, flatten out and fold up
```

Socks: Match and fold. Don't do the "fold and flip" method, as it stretches the elastic and shortens their life span.

 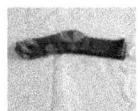  

Do not flip

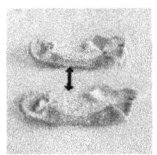 

Final Rule: Keep it clean. Keep it tidy. Your environment reflects your life. If your room is a disaster, your mind probably is too. **Start now.**

Kitchen Combat: Essential Cooking Tips

You have to eat, and relying solely on the cafeteria is a sign of weakness (and a quick way to pack on the Freshman 15). Learn these basic kitchen rules. They are the difference between a decent meal and setting off the fire alarm.

The Stove & Safety Mandates

- Gear Up Smart: Buy medium-priced cookware. Do *not* buy the cheapest thing. If your skillet doesn't sit flat on the burner, you're going to have hot spots and chaos. Invest a little.
- Spice is Life (and Flavor): Keep salt, pepper, and your favorite spices stocked. Bland food is a tragedy.
- Eyes on the Prize: NEVER leave anything on the hot plate or stove unattended. This isn't a suggestion; it's a safety protocol. And make it a habit to kill the oven immediately when the food comes out. Fire codes are not a joke.
- No Sticking: Always hit your skillet with a little cooking spray (Pam), butter or oil before frying anything. A stuck mess is a wasted meal.

Noodle & Meat Protocols

- Boil Hard, Then Back Off: Bring water to a complete, furious boil before adding pasta or ingredients. Adding a bit of salt speeds this process up and adds flavor. Once boiling, immediately reduce the heat a little to prevent

a disastrous overflow. Nobody likes scrubbing starch off the stovetop.
- Kill the Pink (Meat Safety): You are not a culinary adventurer. Cook your meat until there is little or no pink showing. Cut into the thickest part to check.
    - Chicken: This is a zero-tolerance zone for undercooking. Bake it at 350°F for an hour, or fry it at a high temperature, turning every three minutes until the center is cooked completely. Don't mess with chicken.
- Bacon Zen: Bacon cooks better on medium heat. It takes longer, but it minimizes splatter, sticking, and smoking out your entire apartment. Patience yields less cleanup.

Egg Hacks (Making It Look Easy)

- Over-Easy (The Flip Challenge): Flipping an over-easy egg is a feat. To firm up the egg whites around the yolk, poke small holes in the whites while they cook. Using a good layer of cooking spray before will help to loosen it. Tilt the pan slightly, slide the egg onto the spatula, and flip it slowly. Cook for one minute more.
    - *Pro Tip:* If you want the yolk cooked, press down gently on the egg with the spatula once flipped, to force the yolk out a bit and cook for an extra minute.
- Scrambled Fluff: Add a small amount of milk to the egg mixture before cooking. This makes them lighter and fluffier. Throw in meat, cheese, and veggies for a solid, healthier breakfast.

- Potato Hack: Poke holes in both sides of the potato with a fork and microwave 5-8 minutes on high or until soft.

The Grilled Sandwich Blueprint

Grilled cheese is a necessity. Make it right.

1. Butter Up: Butter both outside pieces of the bread.
2. Heat Check: Turn the burner to medium and wait.
3. The Sizzle: Put one buttered piece on the pan. When it sizzles, it's hot enough. Add the cheese, then the top piece (butter side up).
4. The Flip: Once the first side is nicely brown (1-2 minutes), use your spatula and pointer finger to quickly flip the sandwich, keeping the bread pieces aligned.
5. Grill the second side for a minute or two until brown.
- *Meat Warning:* If adding meat, heat it up first in the microwave and drain the grease *before* adding it to the sandwich, or you will end up with a soggy failure.

Potato Frying (The Grease Trap Avoidance)

Frying potatoes (like home fries) can be tricky.

- Oil and Heat: Use plenty of oil and crank the heat to medium high temperature. Add potatoes when the oil is almost boiling.

- Frozen Potato Caution: BE CAREFUL if using frozen potatoes. They will splatter wildly. If using frozen, add them to cool oil, then put the pan on the burner and raise the heat.
- Drain Fast: Let potatoes brown completely on one side before flipping. Once they are done, get them out of the hot oil immediately and drain them on a paper towel. If you leave them sitting in the hot grease and turn the heat down, they will absorb it all. Greasy, unhealthy, and gross.

Baking & Stirring

- Pre-Heat, Dummy: Pre-heat the oven before putting anything in. Failure to do so screws up baking time and guarantees an undercooked mess. Follow the directions, and it will be cake. Always good practice to rotate what you are baking 180 degrees half way through cook time to ensure even baking.
- The Stirring Technique: When stirring things on the stove, move from the center in circles. Do not let the spoon scrape the sides, or you'll mash whatever you're cooking there. Occasionally scrape the outside accumulation back into the mix.

Sample Shopping List for a Month (Fridge and Freezer Needed)

($200.00-$320.00)

2-4 lbs Hamburger (repackage into single portions and freeze)
2-4 lbs Chicken (repackage into single portions and freeze)
2 lbs. Fish, Pork or Sausage or other protein
Hot Dogs (repackage into single portions and freeze)
Bacon (repackage into single portions and freeze)
Lunchmeats (2-3 diff kinds based on lunches and meals)
1 head Lettuce & 2 Tomatoes (Buy weekly so they don't spoil)
Onion
Cucumber
Garlic (1 clump)
Fruits (2-3 different), (Buy weekly so they don't spoil)
1 lb. box Spaghetti
1 lb. box Elbow Macaroni Noodles
Butter
Eggs
Cheese
Bread (2 loaves-multi-grain is best). Freeze one loaf for second week)
Bagels
Muffins
Waffles (Frozen)
1- Large Jar of Italian Sauce "Prego or Ragu etc."
Canned or Frozen Veggies for side dishes
Canned Ravioli or SpaghettiOs etc. (quick snacks)
Ramen Noodles or Soup Cups
Pickles (Favorite kind for sandwiches etc.)
A couple sweet items like "Little Debbie" or Donuts or ?
1 Container of Parmesan Cheese
Salad Dressings (Italian Dressing & Ranch)

This list should get you approximately a months' worth of good meals. Does not include totally pigging out. This is based on normal portions and average standard calories.

The next section introduces you to several decent, easy to make recipes that will not break the bank. Some are 5 minute recipes, some take longer but all of them have easy to follow recipes and a list of ingredients to make them a success. Note. Some of the recipes are intended for students that live off campus in an apartment or house that has a stove and a larger fridge and freezer to store the food correctly.

Quick Meals in Minutes

Meals in 5 Minutes

K's Grilled Cheese & Tomato Soup

Ingredients: American or whatever cheese you like
Dill Pickles
Potato Chips
Bread & butter
1 can of Tomato soup
Directions: Prep time-5 Minutes

Butter the two outside sides of the sandwich while the skillet is reaching medium heat.

Put the bread in the skillet butter side down (skillets usually can only make two sandwiches at a time). Add the cheese. Grill both sides until brown and cheese melts. Finish grilling the other two and you are good to go. Serve hot off the grill with your favorite soup to finish out the meal.

Serve with Potato chips and a dill pickle.

Variations include:

Add your favorite lunch meat to the grilled cheese to add protein.

Ramen Max

Ingredients: Package of Favorite Ramen Noodles

1/4 Bag frozen mixed vegetables

Directions: Prep time-5 Minutes

Add frozen veggies to the boiling water before you put in the noodles. Let the veggies get done, then add a bit more water and the noodles and packet of flavoring. This will make a good hearty meal for under a dollar. Tastes a lot better too when you can actually sink your teeth into the veggies. Try it, you will never eat plain ramen again.

You can also add protein by dicing up some lunchmeat like ham or turkey and add it in too. You can add tuna to add calories to the ramen. This also makes Ramen a real meal.

Variations include:

Add your favorite lunch meat or an egg.

Add hot sauce to spice it up a bit, or tabasco sauce.

Add hot mustard left over from your Chinese night and really spice it up.

Add a dollop of sour cream or ranch dressing to your noodles and mix thoroughly. This changes the whole watery consistency and makes the broth creamy. It is great in the chicken and beef flavors.

Add tabasco or hot sauce to spice it up a bit

All of these options turn a 50 cent Ramen Pack into a good meal that will fool the best of the Ramen Eaters.

Chicago Dogs

Turn a regular dog into a masterpiece

Ingredients:　　Hot Dogs (preferably Hebrew National)
　　　　　　　　Dill Pickles or small hot peppers.
　　　　　　　　Sauerkraut & onions
　　　　　　　　Tomato slices
　　　　　　　　poppy seed hot dog buns
Directions:　　　Prep time-5 Minutes

Boil the hot dogs on high until ready and reduce to low until serving them.

Place hot dogs on buns and add the condiments. To make a real Chicago dog, add ketchup, mustard, sauerkraut, onions, a couple thin tomato slices and a long dill pickle or pepper. . Enjoy... It is excellent!

If you don't like the condiments I have suggested, make it your own way.

Serve with Potato chips, frozen fries or onion rings to make it a full meal.

Meals in 10 Minutes

Ye old French Dip Sandwiches
Makes 4 Large Sandwiches

Ingredients:	1 lb. sliced Roast Beef
	4 slices of Provolone cheese
	1 packet Ajus mix
	Dill Pickle
	Potato Chips
	4 Big Rolls or Buns (Bread gets too soggy)
Directions:	Prep time-10 Minutes

Follow the directions on the Ajus packet and get it simmering in a large skillet. Get the meat separated and add to the heating Ajus. Heat on medium heat until it bubbles, stirring occasionally. Reduce heat to low and simmer. The meat will look all wrinkly and that is normal. It is cooking all the fat into the juice.

Butter the insides of all the rolls and put butter side up on a flat baking tray or right on the top rack in the oven. Brown the rolls for only a few minutes with the broiler. Do not leave the room. It only takes a couple minutes to brown them, but only seconds to burn them. We don't want that. Pay attention.

Remove the rolls from the oven. Divide the meat up evenly on the bottom side of each bun and add a slice of provolone on top. Put back into the oven on broil for a minute or two until the cheese is melted. Take out of the oven, flip the lids on and serve. Cutting sandwiches in half makes it easier to dip.

Scoop the remaining Ajus into 4 small containers to dip the sandwiches into. Serve with Potato chips and a dill pickle.

Italian Sausage Sandwiches

Meal in 10 Minutes (after cooking the sausage)

Ingredients: Italian sausage links
 4 slices of Provolone cheese
 Lettuce & tomato
 Dill Pickle
 Potato Chips
 4 Big Rolls or Buns (Bread gets too soggy)

Directions: Prep time-20-30 Minutes

Brown the sausage in the oven for a half hour or so until it is cooked through. Remove from the oven and slice in half. Put mustard on the bottom side of the bun and put the sausage on it. Put mayo on the top side, load up with lettuce and tomato and enjoy. It is a wonderful blend of spices and with the hot sausage and the cold condiments...it is great.

Serve with chips, a pickle and a soda. Fantastic game day meal.

Also serve with baked beans or potato salad or pasta salad to make a real meal of it. Don't forget the desert. Brownies are awesome with this.

Standard BLTs (10 minutes after cooking Bacon)

Ingredients:	Bacon
	Lettuce & tomato
	Dill Pickle
	Potato Chips
	Lightly Toasted Bread
Directions:	Prep time 10 Minutes

Fry the bacon until crisp. Make your toast. Put mayo on one side with lettuce and tomato and mustard on the bacon side. Salt and pepper and serve. It is simple and tasty.

Serve with chips, a pickle and a soda. Or make a meal and add potato salad or pasta salad and desert.

Remember, you can cook the bacon ahead of time and reheat it to add to the sandwiches. Also good cold.

Mac and Cheese Plus

Ingredients:	Macaroni & Cheese
	And anything you want to add…
	Salt and Pepper
Directions:	Prep time 10 Minutes

Make your Mac N' Cheese and be prepared to have all added stuff prepared and cooked so you can add it when the Mac n cheese is done. Mix in ham and peas as one suggestion. Mix in diced beef and a can of mushrooms. Throw in some chicken and celery. These are all fantastic combinations to be thrown in. If you like fish better, throw in some tuna and top with potato chips. You could also throw in some fish sticks and serve with the mac and cheese. If you are into veggies, throw in all the veggies you got. They all taste great with the mac and cheese. Once again, make sure all other stuff is cooked completely, and add as soon as the noodles are drained. Poor in the cheese, mix and serve.

Serve all of these with a salad and bread for a full meal.

Special Recipe for Tartar Sauce for fish sticks or breaded fish.

Tarter Sauce:	4 spoonful's of mayo (1/4 cup)
	a dime size dab of mustard
	sweet pickle relish to taste. More the better
	a squeeze of lemon juice.
	*makes a little more than a 1/4 cup.
Directions:	Mix thoroughly and serve when ready.

Day or Night Spanish Eggs:

This recipe is simple, fast, and uses minimal gear. It's perfect for fueling up before a morning class or a late-night study grind. We're turning simple eggs into a portable, cheesy survival tool.

Ingredients (The Core Loadout)

- **Eggs** (Your primary protein source)
- **Flour Tortillas** (The delivery vehicle)
- Shredded **Cheddar Cheese** (The glue and flavor)
- **Salsa** (Mandatory zest)
- **Butter** (For flavor and crisping)

Prep and Heat

1. **Butter the Shell:** Lightly butter one side of each flour tortilla and set them aside.
2. **Oven Hack (Optional):** If you have an oven, preheat it to **250°F** now just to warm the tortillas. If not, you can microwave them for 10 seconds or skip this step.
3. **Pan Heat:** Get your skillet onto a medium-high burner. Hit the pan with a layer of Pam or cooking oil.

The Egg Assault (Over-Easy Style)

1. **Crack and Commit:** Once the pan is hot, crack two eggs on the side of the skillet. Separate the shell slowly using your thumbs to keep the yolk intact. **Do not break the yolk yet.** If it breaks, don't panic, just keep the egg somewhat together.
2. **Solidify the Whites:** Let the eggs cook until all the clear white is opaque. To speed this up, use the **Chapter 8**

> **Pro Tip:** poke small holes in the white part around the yolk. This firms up the egg quickly.

3. **Flip it:** Once the white is firm, slide your spatula under the egg and flip it carefully.
4. **Warm the Tortillas:** Now that the eggs are flipped, throw the tortillas into the oven (or microwave) for a few minutes to soften.

Customizing the Yolk (Your Choice)

- **Cooked Through (Clean Eating):** After the eggs have cooked on the second side for a couple of minutes, press down firmly on the center yolk to break it. This allows it to cook completely.
- **Runny (Messy & Tasty):** If you prefer a messy, delicious, runny yolk, just cook normally and **do not break the yolk.**

Assembly and Devour

1. **Extract:** Once the eggs and tortillas are done, remove the tortillas.
2. **Load:** Place the eggs inside the center of the tortilla, dividing them evenly.
3. **Cheese and Heat:** Sprinkle generously with cheddar cheese. The heat from the eggs will start to melt the cheese..
4. **The Finisher:** Add your favorite salsa or hot sauce.
5. **Roll and Conquer:** Roll the tortilla up tight. ¡**Whaaaalaa! Spanish Eggs.** *Bueno.*
- **Serve With:** Hashbrowns, juice, or fruit—whenever the hell you need a quick meal.

Meals in 20 Minutes

These 20-minute meals will require a stove top or oven.

K's Goulash-Makes 8 Huge Servings

Ingredients: 1 lb. Ground Hamburger
1 lb. Box or Bag of Elbow Macaroni
1 jar Italian Sauce (Prego with Meat)
Salt (Garlic salt too if possible) and Pepper
Parmesan Cheese

Directions: Prep time-20 Minutes

Brown the hamburger in a skillet on medium-high heat, breaking up into ground chunks once it starts to sizzle. Add a dash of salt and pepper to the meat as it cooks through. Make sure to let it cook for a few minutes once there is no pink showing. This will guarantee it cooks long enough at a high enough temperature. After a few minutes drain the grease in a strainer (or paper towel) in the sink and put the ground hamburger back in the skillet.

Pour the jar of Italian sauce into the meat and simmer on low heat stirring occasionally until noodles are ready.

Start Boiling the water for the noodles (You can start it sooner if it takes longer for the pasta to cook). Fill the largest pan you got with 3/4 of water. Put on high heat until it boils. Add a slight bit of salt to the water and a drip of cooking oil. This will speed up the boiling process, add flavor to the noodles and help with the sticking of noodles. Read directions on the pasta to make sure you time the noodles to be done last. Once noodles are done and drained, put them back in the big pot and add the meat sauce. Add salt, pepper and parmesan cheese and mix gently together. Serve with garlic bread and salad.

Garlic bread: Spread a thin layer of butter, a thin sprinkle of garlic salt and a thin layer of Parmesan cheese. If you really want to get fancy, put a dash of parsley. Now that's Italian. Good salad: Regular Iceberg lettuce, cucumber and red onion with croutons topped with Good Seasons Italian dressing. Wow what a meal.

Poor Man Tacos or Nachos

Makes 12-16 Tacos or Tons of Nachos

Ingredients:	1 lb. Ground Hamburger

1 Can Pork n Beans

1 packet taco seasoning

lettuce & Tomato diced

shredded cheese

Hot Sauce

Taco Shells or Tortilla chips

Directions:	Prep time-15-20 Minutes

Brown the hamburger in a skillet on medium high heat breaking up into ground chunks once it starts to sizzle. Add a dash of salt and pepper to the meat as it cooks through. Make sure to let it cook for a few minutes once there is no pink showing. This will guarantee it cooks long enough at a high enough temperature. After a few minutes drain the grease in a strainer (or paper towel) in the sink and put the ground hamburger back in the skillet.

Pour the can of pork 'n' beans into the hamburger and stir in the taco seasoning and the correct amount of water for the seasoning. Heat on medium heat until it bubbles, stirring occasionally. Reduce heat to low and simmer.

While the hamburger mixture is cooking, shred the lettuce, tomato and cheese. Add a small amount of Italian dressing to the Lettuce and Tomato Mixture to give it a tangy layer of taste. I use Good Seasons Italian Mix and just use a tablespoon. Do not put too much dressing on the mixture.

Put taco shells from the box in the oven for 5 minutes while preparing toppings. If you want more authentic shells, use flat corn tortillas and fry them in a small amount of oil and fold them over once they are cooked on both sides. The longer you cook them the crunchier they get. Add a dash of salt to them as they are cooking.

Once everything is complete, build the tacos with a layer of cheese at the bottom, then meat mixture, then lettuce and tomato mixture, and top it off with some salsa. Enjoy!

Alternate Use of Hamburger Mixture for Nachos...

Toss down some tortilla chips, dump on the meat mixture and cheese and heat in the oven for 5 minutes. Add the cold toppings and you will enjoy the same treat even quicker. Enjoy.

Sour cream/Guacamole always adds that special touch if you can afford it.

*The reason they are called poor man tacos is because you add the beans to make the meat stretch further. You can always cut the recipe in half or a quarter to make a smaller amount

---

NY Grilled Pastrami Melt

Makes 4 Large Sandwiches

Ingredients:	1 lb. sliced Pastrami

4 slices of Swiss Cheese

1 small can sauerkraut

Dill Pickles

Potato Chips

Bread (Marbled Rye preferred)

Directions:	Prep time-15 Minutes

Get the meat separated and heat in a skillet on medium heat for 5 minutes. Take the pastrami out of the skillet and put it on a dish nearby, and divide it into 4 even piles.

While cooking the meat, butter the two outside sides of each sandwich to begin grilling like a grilled cheese sandwich.

Clean the skillet and put back on the burner on medium heat. Add 2 pieces of bread butter side down (skillets usually can only make two sandwiches at a time). Load each slice of bread up with a pile of pastrami, a pile of kraut and a slice of Swiss cheese. Put the top piece of bread on the butter side out and start grilling. Grill both sides until brown and cheese is melting. Finish grilling the other two and you are good to go.

Serve with Potato chips and a dill pickle.

Special Dressing for a sandwich:

> 3 tablespoons of Mayo
>
> 1 Tablespoon Ketchup
>
> 1 tablespoon sweet pickle relish.

Makes this an authentic NY pastrami on rye sandwich. Wow

Colorado Chili

Ingredients:
- 1 lb. Ground Hamburger
- 1 can stewed tomatoes
- 1 packet chili seasoning
- 1 large can of Spicy Chili Beans w/juice
- 2 cans of Pinto Beans with juice
- 1 can of kidney beans (Strained)
- 1 cup diced onions.

Directions: Prep time-20 Minutes, Cooking time 1-2 hours.

Brown the hamburger in a skillet on medium high heat breaking up into ground chunks once it starts to sizzle. Add a dash of salt and pepper to the meat as it cooks through. Make sure to let it cook for a few minutes once there is no pink showing. This will guarantee it cooks long enough at a high enough temperature.

After a few minutes drain the grease in a strainer (or paper towel) in the sink and put the ground hamburger in a Cooking pot. Pour in all other ingredients, and enough water to cover all ingredients and bring to a boil, stirring occasionally for the first 5 minutes or so. Reduce heat and cook for an hour. The longer it simmers on low the better it tastes. Serve with Fritos, cheese, tortillas, crackers and even a dash of sour cream. Good stuff.

This makes 10 servings so you can have it later on your chili dogs and chili burgers. If you have any left after that, drizzle on tortilla chips and have some chili nachos. Wow 3 great meals from one pot of chili.

Using leftover Chili is Quick and Easy!

Super Chili Dogs & Chili Burgers

Ingredients: Hot Dogs (preferably Hebrew National)

or Hamburger patties

hotdog/hamburger buns

Pre-cooked chili

shredded cheddar or American cheese slices

Directions: Prep time-10 Minutes

Boil the hot dogs on high until ready and reduce to low until serving them or fry your hamburgers and leave warm in the skillet. Heat up leftover chili in a pan on the stove.

Butter the insides of the hot dog/hamburger buns and place hot buns on a cookie sheet. Broil on the top rack until brown. Do not leave the buns in. Watch them closely. We want them toasted, not burnt. When buns are ready, place them open face on a plate. Cut the hot dog in half and lay each half on each half of the bun or half a hamburger. Smother with chili, top with cheese and serve. I like to add onions, a little ketchup on top with a few dabs of mustard here and there, but prepare as you like. I also put a handful of French fries on top to finish it off. This is a great, quick meal.

Tattor-tot Casserole

Ingredients: 1 lb. Ground Hamburger

1/2 bag of tater tots

1 can cream of mushroom soup

Half bag of mixed vegetables

Shredded Cheddar cheese

Salt and Pepper

Directions: Prep time-20 Minutes, Cooking time 1 hour.

Brown the hamburger in a skillet on medium high heat breaking up into ground chunks once it starts to sizzle. Add a dash of salt and pepper to the meat as it cooks through. Make sure to let it cook for a few minutes once there is no pink showing. This will guarantee it cooks long enough at a high enough temperature. After a few minutes, drain the grease in a strainer (or paper towel) in the sink and put the ground hamburger in a medium sized baking dish. Add the mixed vegetables and soup and mix together. Cover with shredded cheddar cheese.

Put the tater tots on top of the mixture and bake in the oven on the specified temperature for the tater-tots usually 20 minutes. Once the tators are nice and brown, remove from the oven. Let stand for 5 minutes before serving.

This is a good meal to cook for that special someone that is cheap, looks good and tastes great.

K's Quick Spaghetti

Ingredients: 1 lb. Ground Hamburger

1 lb. Box or Spaghetti

1 jar Italian Sauce (Prego)

Salt (Garlic salt too if possible) and Pepper

Parmesan Cheese

Directions: Prep time-20 Minutes

Brown the hamburger in a skillet on medium high heat breaking up into ground chunks once it starts to sizzle. Add a dash of salt and pepper to the meat as it cooks through. Make sure to let it cook for a few minutes once there is no pink showing. This will guarantee it cooks long enough at a high enough temperature. After a few minutes drain the grease in a strainer (or paper towel) in the sink and put the ground hamburger back in the skillet.

Pour the jar of Italian sauce into the meat and simmer on low heat stirring occasionally until the noodles are ready.

Start Boiling the water for the noodles (You can start it sooner if it takes longer for the pasta to cook). Fill the largest pan you got with 3/4 of water. Put on high heat until it boils. Add a slight bit of salt to the water and drip of cooking oil. This will initiate the boiling process, add flavor to the noodles and help with the sticking of noodles. Read directions on the pasta to make sure you time the noodles to be done last and add the other ingredients to them at the end. This ensures the noodles are cooked properly.

Once noodles are done and drained, put them back in the big pot and add the meat sauce. Add salt, pepper and parmesan cheese and mix gently together. Serve with garlic bread and salad.

The next day have it for lunch. It may be a little dry, but add a little sprinkle of water, a few drops of ketchup, mix together and microwave. It is great the second day too.

You can substitute the spaghetti noodles for elbow noodles and call it Goulash, too.

The 3-Ingredient Shredded Chicken

This base chicken is incredibly versatile and can be used for tacos, sandwiches, salads, or mixed with rice/pasta.

Ingredients

- 2 large **Chicken Breasts** (or 3 thighs)
- 1 can (14 oz) of **Chicken Broth** (low sodium)
- 1 packet of **Taco Seasoning** (or your favorite seasoning blend: Italian, Ranch, etc.)

Cooking Instructions (Hot Plate/Stovetop)

1. **Sauté:** Cut the chicken breasts into 2-inch chunks (this speeds cooking). In a pot or deep skillet, lightly coat the bottom with oil. Sauté the chicken for 2-3 minutes until lightly browned on the outside.
2. **Simmer:** Pour in the chicken broth and sprinkle in the seasoning packet. Bring the liquid to a simmer over medium-high heat.
3. **Cook & Shred:** Reduce the heat to medium-low, cover the pot, and let it simmer for **20–25 minutes**, or until the chicken shreds easily with a fork.
4. **Shred:** Remove the chicken from the liquid and shred it using two forks. Mix the shredded chicken back into a bit of the leftover broth for moisture.
5. **Use It:** Serve over rice, in tortillas, or put it on a sandwich.

Quick-Fry Lemon Pepper Chicken

This is a fast dinner that only requires a skillet and a hot plate.

Ingredients

- 1 large **Chicken Breast**, sliced horizontally into 3 thin cutlets
- 1 tablespoon **Olive Oil** or cooking spray
- 1 teaspoon **Lemon Pepper Seasoning**
- $1/2$ teaspoon **Garlic Powder**
- Pinch of **Salt**

Cooking Instructions (Hot Plate/Stovetop)

1. **Prep:** Place the thin chicken cutlets on a plate. Sprinkle generously on both sides with lemon pepper, garlic powder, and salt.
2. **Heat:** Set your skillet or pan over medium-high heat and add the olive oil or cooking spray.
3. **Sear:** Carefully place the cutlets in the hot pan (they should sizzle immediately). Do not overcrowd the pan.
4. **Cook:** Cook for **6–8 minutes total**, flipping once halfway through. Since the cutlets are thin, they cook quickly. Check the thickest piece to ensure it is white all the way through.
5. **Serve:** Serve immediately with a side salad or quick-cooking pasta.

Sheet Pan Chicken and Veggies

(Oven Required)

If you have access to an oven, this is the easiest way to make a complete, healthy meal with minimal cleanup.

Ingredients

- 2 large **Chicken Breasts** (cut into 1-inch cubes)
- 1 bag (16 oz) of **Frozen Broccoli Florets** (or chopped fresh potatoes/carrots)
- 2 tablespoons **Olive Oil**
- 1 teaspoon **Italian Seasoning**
- 1/2 teaspoon **Salt** and **Pepper**
- 1-2 cloves **Garlic**, minced (optional, use garlic powder if you don't have fresh)

Cooking Instructions (Oven)

1. **Preheat:** Preheat your oven to **400°F**. Line a sheet pan with aluminum foil for zero cleanup.
2. **Toss:** In a large bowl, combine the cubed chicken and the frozen vegetables. Drizzle with olive oil, Italian seasoning, salt, pepper, and garlic. Toss until everything is evenly coated.
3. **Spread:** Dump the contents of the bowl onto the lined sheet pan and spread it out into a single layer.
4. **Roast:** Bake for **25–30 minutes**, stirring the mixture halfway through, until the chicken is golden and cooked completely through (no pink!) and the vegetables are tender.
5. **Serve:** Eat straight off the pan, or divide into containers for meal prep.

Essential Cooking Tip Reminder

- **Safety:** Always check the thickest part of the chicken. If it is still pink, keep cooking!
- **Cleanup:** Soak pans immediately. Don't let the mess harden, as Chapter 8 taught you.

Standard Shopping List-Every 3-6 Months

- Laundry Detergent
- Stain Stick
- Fabric Softener
- Dryer Sheets
- Cleansing Soap
- Paper Towels
- Napkins
- Paper Plates
- Toilet Paper
- Shaving Cream

- Razors
- Lotion
- Deodorant
- Aftershave/cologne/perfume
- Acne remedies
- Disinfectant hand soap
- Salt & Pepper
- Spices
- Worcestershire sauce
- toothpicks
- Band-Aides
- Aspirin (other cold & flu medicines)
- Cough Drops
- Chap Stick
- Nail clippers

*Hopefully you got your parents to buy the first round of these supplies and they bought it in bulk because after that, you are probably on your own and you'll have to buy the minimum to get you by for at least a couple months. Probably for the first time you will realize how expensive this crap is and start conserving and being wise about usage and wasting product. Be smart about what you buy, use it sparingly and it will last longer. Good luck.

Check out the female version.

https://www.amazon.com/dp/B0GS9BKKLC

www.ingramcontent.com/pod-product-compliance
Lightning Source LLC
Chambersburg PA
CBHW060854050426
42453CB00008B/979